REA

ACPL ITEM
DISCARDED

Testimonials from students, parents, and educators

"You should try as hard as possible to keep your parents from coming to school. It's so embarrassing."
          –Student

"I was embarrassed to have my mom come to school, so I stopped acting up, and then my grades went from Ds and Fs to As and Bs."
          –Student

"Mr. Lazares effectively pleads his case for a 'triangle' approach—child, parent, school—of connected individuals as the only means of raising our children today.

Parents, take this book to your administrators. Accept nothing less than the passion and commitment displayed by Mr. Lazares for your own children!"
          –Parent

"Mr. Lazares's ideas and practice are fantastic!"
          –Parent

"The stories and suggestions are important for each of us and have so much value!"
          –Parent

"If only more administrators, teachers, and parents would follow Mr. Lazares's philosophy, what a better school environment we would have."
          –Clergyman

Please, Don't Call My Mother!

How Parents and Schools Can Team Up to Get Kids Back on Track

Please, Don't Call My Mother!

How Parents and Schools Can Team Up to Get Kids Back on Track

Revised Edition

John Lazares, M.Ed.

with Coleen Armstrong

PARENTING PRESS, INC.

Seattle | Washington

Designed by Magrit Baurecht Design
Printed in the United States of America

Library of Congress Cataloging-in-Publication Data
Lazares, John, 1949-
    Please don't call my mother! : how parents and
    schools can team up to get kids back on track /
    by John Lazares and Coleen Armstrong.— Rev.ed.
        p. cm.
    Includes index.
    ISBN 1-884734-62-6 (lib. bdg.) — ISBN 1-884734-61-8
    (pbk.)
    1. School discipline. 2. Education — Parent
    participation. I. Armstrong, Coleen, 1946-
    II. Title.

        LB3012.L39   2002
        373.15 — dc21

                                              2001059145

Parenting Press, Inc.
P.O. Box 75267, Seattle, Washington 98125

Telephone (206) 364-2900 | www.ParentingPress.com

Contents

1

The Parental Intervention Plan (PIP)

"Oh, no," I groaned. "Not you again."

The face was familiar. Too familiar. This eighth grader had been sent to my office, in fact, nearly every day since school had begun. His list of transgressions read like our junior high Code of Conduct itself. He'd skipped school, been tardy to class, sassed his teachers, and started fights. Now he slouched in his chair across from my desk and stared sullenly at his feet.

"What were you doing this time?" I asked.

He shrugged and tried to look bored. "Just messing around, I guess."

Messing around? That could mean anything from tossing a wad of paper to hanging from a light fixture. In this case, it was probably closer to the latter. I sighed.

We'd been through the whole route of detentions and suspensions. I'd tried warning, advising, lecturing. Nothing worked. I felt helpless.

As I wrote out the required suspension forms for what seemed like the fifteenth time, I shook my head in exasperation. "Know what I'm going to do the next time you misbehave?" I demanded, my voice rising. "I'm going to call your mother and ask her to sit with you through all of your classes! Maybe she ought to see what we have to put up with every day!"

In twelve years of school administration, I'd seen lots of things. I'd seen students suspended, expelled, even arrested. But I'd never seen anything even closely resembling the panic that suddenly appeared on that eighth grader's face.

"Oh, no, Mr. Lazares," he protested, sitting up straighter in his chair. "Oh, no. You don't have to do that. I'll be good from now on, I promise. I'll do anything. Only . . . please don't call my mother!"

Inside my head, a light switched on.

■ ■ ■

Everyone knows that nowadays schools are forced to deal with offenses that were unheard of forty years ago: Assault, robbery, arson, drug dealing—and now, kids bringing guns to class and, on occasion, killing teachers, administrators, and/or fellow students.

What many people don't realize, however, is that schools can be almost as frustrated with so-called "minor" offenses as with major ones. Because these offenses don't usually hit the newspaper headlines and are committed by ordinary, growing children, most people don't realize how prevalent they are in a typical school day. Principals can't very well call the police every time a kid doesn't turn in his homework, is caught smoking or skipping detention, or when he's repeatedly late for homeroom. We have to deal with most problems according to the school's own discipline code.

Every school has a discipline code whose aim is to help teachers and administrators keep order so that learning can take place. Even in the "best" of schools, the need for discipline exists. The difficulty is that many codes are poorly written and/or poorly communicated. They may talk about prohibiting "disrespect," for example, but what's that? A look? A smile? A refusal to do any work? How about a refusal to show up at all?

Discipline in our schools has grown lax in recent years for several reasons:

- An increased emphasis on individual rights and freedoms;
- Time-consuming due-process procedures which make enforcing a code almost more trouble than it's worth;
- The emotional and moral absence of too many parents who live with their children in a physical sense only and are eager to assume the good-guy role by putting administrators on the defensive.

As long as school personnel and parents stay on opposite sides, enforcing discipline will continue to be a mess. We must begin to work together; it's our only choice.

What we need to incorporate into our schools isn't necessarily a stricter set of rules—but a clearer one. What we need to establish isn't necessarily a stronger front—but a united one.

A Progressive Discipline Code

Many middle school and high schools' discipline codes have recently been rewritten, not only to tighten up on inappropriate behavior, but to become what we now call "progressive." That means students are given progressively stiffer penalties for repeated infractions of the same rule, or for one within the same category or "track." So if your son or daughter comes home and complains, "I just got suspended for leaving my math book in my locker!" you may respond with, "Huh?"

What you want to do instead is ask how many times that's already happened, and why your child keeps on doing it.

A seemingly innocuous act like forgetting to bring a book to class can quickly become a huge annoyance to the teacher who has to put up with it (and who will be later called to account for why Johnny can't pass his proficiency test). Therefore, schools don't allow a student to repeat the same misbehavior and receive the same minor penalty over and over, because that won't change a thing.

Let's say a student is repeatedly tardy to his sixth period class. Maybe he's hanging out too long with his girlfriend in the east wing. The first time it happens, he receives a single detention. The second time, the same. But the third time, he's put into in-school suspension for a day and the fourth time, he's suspended.

So it's not unheard of for a student eventually to be suspended for the very same act that once earned him only a detention or even demerits. Luckily, most kids mend their ways long before that stage. But a few are stubborn, lackadaisical, or just don't mind being suspended.

And that's another problem. We administrators have a love-hate relationship with suspension. It's common punishment in many districts, but it's a far-from-perfect solution. When it's used, everybody loses. The principal, because it makes him or her look helpless in dealing with student discipline. The teacher, because special make-up assignment sheets have to be made, and then he or she must play catch-up when the student finally returns to class. The parents, because they either worry about what their son or daughter is doing home alone— or else they're irritated by the kid's very presence. And the student, of course, because he or she is either sitting on the couch watching bad television, or out wandering the streets and shopping malls, instead of in school getting an education.

That's how in-school suspension (ISS) originated, by the way, because of our collective disenchantment. Instead of being dumped onto the streets, students now sit through an all-day study hall.

They are suspended from classes, but not from school. This keeps parents and teachers happier, and it removes the kids' notion that suspensions are really paid vacations. ISS is one last step before out-of-school suspension (OSS). There, at least within a supervised framework, students can keep plugging away at their assignments.

Still, the system doesn't always work as well as we'd like it to, and we know it. Occasionally, students don't mind ISS, for example, because they feel it's easier than attending classes. Once in a while, they'll even push the system and get suspended out of school deliberately, just to accompany their friends who are already suspended or expelled.

With the seed of an idea already germinating in my mind, I felt certain I could address all of the defects in the suspension system at once. I just had to find a way to implement my idea.

■ ■ ■

I'd left Todd the Troublemaker still sitting in his chair across from my desk. I'd been silent for several moments while my mind raced. Todd watched me uneasily.

Suddenly I sprang into action. I picked up the telephone receiver, tossed it into the air, chuckled, and punched out the digits of a number I already knew by heart. Then, still smiling, I handed the receiver to Todd.

He took it from me with a labored sigh. He knew what was expected of him. It was a favorite tactic of mine to have the students themselves call their parents when they were about to be suspended. It removed the school from the role of the bad guy, and placed the blame where it rightfully belonged . . . on the student.

"Mama, . . ." I heard Todd begin. I tried to suppress a grin. It never failed. The hardest cases reverted to baby-hood when they had to face their own parents with the consequences of what they'd done.

Now Todd was stammering out his story, making chopped liver of the whole thing. Finally, I took pity on him and held out my hand for the receiver.

"Hi, Mrs. Wyatt, this is John Lazares," I said. I could have called her Irene if I'd wanted to; through Todd we knew each other pretty well.

"Yes, he's been suspended again, this time for three days. . . . I know that. . . . Yes, I know it's a problem for you. . . . Yes. . . . Tell you what." I took a deep breath. "I'll take the suspension away if you'll come in and sit with him all day. . . . No, just one morning and afternoon. Yes, of course I mean it."

A minute later I replaced the telephone receiver, sat down, and leaned back in my chair. "Todd," I said to the astonished boy before me whose mouth was literally hang-ing open, "tomorrow your mother is coming to school."

Taking Care of Business

A well-written school discipline code has several traits that make it workable. First, its regulations and penalties are clearly spelled out. Students can never claim that what they've done isn't technically against any rule. Don't laugh; a discipline code that isn't air-tight will leave holes wide enough for any teenager to drive a truck through if we let him. It's part of our job not to let him.

Second, it's communicated thoroughly to the student body. In many schools, each student is given a folder with the code printed inside on the first day of school. Nobody can claim later that he didn't know what would happen if he brought a radio to class, tried to store drugs in her locker, or grabbed a quick smoke behind the gymnasium. (Many schools have lately been forced to have every student sign a sheet indicating he or she has received said policy in writing—otherwise the student can insist when caught doing something wrong that he or she has never seen the code!)

Third, it involves monitoring by a full-time administrator. His or her primary job is to keep track of each student's disciplinary progress.

I personally favor a file-card system. Each student that I or my assistant saw during my principalship had a card which listed the date, time, and nature of every offense. (When we finished one card, we simply started another.) Everything was documented, even small incidents like being sent to the office by a teacher just to mellow out—which may or may not have resulted in any punishment.

At a mere glance, I could see that the student sitting before me had been repeatedly insolent to his math and science teachers, or that he had an interesting tendency to start fights in the hallways. It's tough for a student (or his parents) to argue that he hasn't been in "all that much" trouble when shown a long list of clearly documented offenses. It's tough to maintain that a certain teacher has it in for him when a principal points out a whole series of offenses in different classrooms at opposite ends of a large building.

Fourth, a successful discipline code involves parents. Parents should be called on the phone and informed of every incident, even if the punishment is only demerits. They should also be warned at every step concerning the penalty for the next infraction. A principal's ultimate goal should be no surprised parents—ever. A parent should never express astonishment that his child has just been suspended from school. What you don't want to hear is, "Why didn't you tell us he was having problems? We had no idea!" Regular phone calls, with the dates noted on the student's file card, will eliminate this possibility.

■ ■ ■

Mrs. Wyatt was just the kind of parent I loved to see in my office: Cheerful, cooperative, anxious to do just about anything to help her son get along better in school. Todd's misbehaving, we both felt, was a temporary adolescent condition, something he'd eventually grow out of. Still, as we shook our heads together in commiseration, we both added that we hoped he'd grow out of it soon.

Now there was a way, I thought, to speed up that process. Mrs. Wyatt would make an ideal test case for what I was already calling in my mind a Parental Intervention Plan.

Sitting together in my office the following morning, I told Mrs. Wyatt that the procedure was really quite simple. Todd's teachers had all been notified that I was trying a disciplinary experiment. Mrs. Wyatt would be seated next to her son in every class—but she wouldn't be called on or expected to help with any assignments. She wouldn't be drafted into becoming a teacher's aide. She'd merely be an observer, and hopefully her presence would temper Todd's usual ebullience.

Mrs. Wyatt said it all sounded fine to her. She was eager to get started. I escorted her to Todd's homeroom, where we waited in the hallway for the first bell.

An hour or so later I decided to see how things were

going. I sauntered upstairs to Todd's second period math class. As I poked my head in the doorway, I sensed immediately that something in the room was different. The atmosphere seemed electric, in fact, supercharged! Although the teacher was conducting her usual lesson at the board, something else was definitely out-of-the-ordinary. For once, she had the complete, silent, and rapt attention of every single person in the room.

Mrs. Wyatt was sitting in the last seat near the window, watching the teacher intently. Todd was sitting next to her, staring straight ahead, trying very hard not to catch anyone's eye. His classmates were doing the same, trying hard not to look at him either—but I saw two or three sneaking occasional glances in his direction.

I walked back to my office, grinning. I had discovered the key to dealing with the minor (and sometimes persistent) transgressions of ordinary students—parental intervention!

After school that day, I sat down with Mrs. Wyatt once more. She'd been very impressed, she told me, with the smoothness of our school's operation and with the caliber of teaching she'd witnessed. Todd, she reported, had been very subdued all day; in fact, she'd hardly heard a peep from him. "Anything else?" I asked after a moment.

"Yes," Mrs. Wyatt sighed. "I think all of your teachers deserve raises."

Fringe Benefits

Within the next two weeks I had twenty more parents come to school for a day. By then the teachers were thoroughly accustomed to having such visitors, and they shared many a private chuckle over how we'd finally managed to get parents to take an interest in their children's education. Nobody seemed particularly self-conscious about being observed by adults; in fact, they rather enjoyed it. The new, receptive audience was gratifying, and the parents' interest seemed to rub off. Student attention spans had actually improved.

Parents, I found, were especially eager to share their insights at the end of the school day. And without exception, their reactions and comments were positive. "I had no idea," one father exclaimed, "that teaching was such hard work!" "You're doing a far better job here than the public realizes," said another.

Kids' motivation in class also rose; in fact, it soared. Students whose parents were sitting with them in class didn't want it to happen ever again. Those who hadn't yet had the privilege could see for themselves that it wasn't a club they particularly wanted to join.

Sometimes one parent's presence became almost a surrogate for others. In an English class, the teacher instructed her group to turn to page 312. A boy who sat without moving was suddenly poked in the arm by his mother. "You heard her," the woman commanded. "Turn the page!" Three other kids sitting nearby overheard her and instinctively obeyed.

At the end of the first two weeks, our usual after-school detention list had dwindled from a daily average of thirty to zero. I received that news with a smile and a shrug. By then I wasn't even surprised.

How did I account for such rapid, unparalleled success? Simple.

Every single kid in my building had heard about Todd that first day. Every single kid went out of his or her way to get a look at The Guy Whose Mother Came to School. Naturally, a few couldn't resist making teasing remarks, but most of them just gaped. They all realized that sheer luck had insulated them against the same embarrassing predicament.

Some time early in the second week, a visiting mother was overheard telling her son, "If I ever have to come back here, I'm going to hold your hand as we walk down the hallway." The story spread, and a collective shudder went through the entire building. The rest of the day passed without a single disciplinary incident.

The "preventive" factor was working.

I guess this is a good time to make it clear that the purpose of the plan isn't the humiliation of children. It's prevention of problems, discipline at an early, manageable stage, and enhancement of the educational process.

A child who's repeatedly in trouble for even minor disciplinary offenses is already forging a clear path for himself. He quickly becomes known to teachers, parents, classmates—and even himself—as a problem. And if that's what he thinks he does best, then he's going to continue doing it. We adults have a responsibility to grab him by the scruff of the neck when he's going the wrong way and set him down on another path. There's no better way to accomplish this than to have parents and teachers doing that "scruff grabbing" together.

The Parental Intervention Plan, or PIP as I call it, has a number of benefits:

- Unlike suspensions, parental visits result in no instruction time being lost. Students are in classrooms where they belong.
- Parents grow more comfortable inside the school building. They no longer hesitate to contact a teacher or a principal about their concerns. Communication and understanding improve on both sides.
- Every time someone has a chance to observe firsthand what's really going on, the school's public image improves. People discover that what they've read in the newspapers about uncontrollable classes and teachers who can't teach isn't happening in their building. If a school is doing its job well in the first place, support for

education in general, and that school in particular, will always increase.

■ A clear message is conveyed to all students: Your parents and teachers are working together now. You can't play games or try to jerk them around. If you tangle with one, then you'll have to tangle with both. See that parent sitting in the third row? That could be your mom, your dad. We've combined our forces to guarantee that you make the most of your educational opportunities.

■ PIP costs the school and district nothing and works with children of all ages. What awesome power!

2

How to Be
a Great Principal

There are two kinds of principals: Office principals and building principals. The office principal sits at his or her desk behind a closed door, filling out forms and dealing with people primarily by e-mail or telephone. The building principal is out patrolling the halls, observing classes, and chatting with everyone from students to custodians.

By now you've probably guessed which one I was.

On Being Visible

I believe that the most important rule of principalship is being visible and accessible, available to hear the concerns of teachers, students, parents, and support staff. People can't always be expected to seek you out; you have to go where they are.

When I was principal (I am now a superintendent of schools), my junior high school, like other schools in the district, had an open-door policy, whereby citizens were welcome to drop by and observe classes at any time. I made it a practice myself to visit classrooms between two and five times daily. Both students and teachers became thoroughly accustomed to seeing visitors (like me) poking their heads through their doors.

My administrative patrols accomplished several purposes:

- First, I was always in touch with my teachers' concerns. If someone had a need or a problem, he or she didn't have to hunt me down after school; he or she could merely wait until my next stop in the classroom. I found teachers more likely to voice their genuine concerns when I came to them, rather than the other way around. I used to carry a little notebook with me and jot down what I needed to do right on the spot. Now I carry a Palm Pilot and a cell phone.

    Not enough chalk, for example, sounds like something that can be placed on a back burner—but it can become a major annoyance to the math teacher in room 315 who is running low. Hand-carrying three fresh boxes within the hour to the person who mentioned it sure beats the embarrassment of having to be reminded of the problem again a week later.

- Second, I was always aware of what was really going on in my building. If a parent called to object to some methodology or subject matter, I could address the concern immediately, without the standard I'll-check-into-this-and-call-you-back-in-two-days routine. It's a real pleasure to be able to tell a parent, "You've heard that Mr. Hill isn't covering World War II in his history class? Well, I was just in that room an hour ago, and it appears you've been misinformed."

- Third, I was always on top of who my best teachers were and why. I saw them in action, so I knew what made them outstanding. I made sure that they received public recognition for their excellent work.

I was also aware of who was marginal and what he or she needed to do to improve, or who was bad and needed to be dismissed. I did everything I could to help teachers improve, and if that didn't work, I sought to get rid of them. (Covering and retaining incompetent teachers does the school and the district a terrible injustice. It frustrates kids, alienates parents, and demoralizes fellow staff members.)

It goes without saying that students benefit from a principal's high visibility too. Kids who see their principal in the hallways and in classrooms soon regard him or her as an approachable person, instead of some nonentity. This makes them more likely to share their problems, and a principal is more likely to sense when trouble is brewing. A principal who patrols the halls between classes and keeps his or her ears open is rarely surprised by a student walkout the day before spring break!

High visibility goes a long way toward eliminating problems, misunderstandings, and grievances. If you're perceived as "being there," then people will grow to view you as being there for them.

On Keeping in Touch

On the rare occasions that I got home before 10:00 p.m., I tended to settle into an easy chair with the telephone right in my lap. That made it easier for me to answer the phone when it rang (it always did) and for me to make the sixty or so phone calls that I made to parents every single week.

Yes, you heard that right. I insisted that each of my teachers stay in touch with parents by making at least five positive calls each week. (E-mails, if you prefer, are just as effective.) And since I never asked teachers to do anything I wouldn't do, I tried to make several times as many myself.

Why? Because the results were worth it.

Consider the predicament of the average parent. Because he or she never hears from the child's school unless the kid has done something wrong, many (thankfully) never hear a word. Those who find it necessary to come to the phone brace themselves for bad news, because that's all they're accustomed to hearing.

Now consider what happens when the child's teacher calls just to tell them he's earned an A on a geography test, or when the principal calls to congratulate them on his making the honor roll.

They're flabbergasted, overjoyed, and very impressed.

What's more, if the teacher or principal needs to call later in the year about something negative, the parents are ten times more cooperative, because the call comes from someone whom they perceive as genuinely concerned about their child's welfare.

On Zero Tolerance

Zero tolerance sounded like a great idea at first. Any student in possession of weapons or illegal drugs on school grounds should be expelled—for at least the rest of the school year, perhaps permanently, and maybe even from every public school in the state. No exceptions, none, not ever.

Most principals, including me, agreed wholeheartedly with this get-tough philosophy.

But then things got out of hand. Out of fear for their children's safety, parents, administrators, and lawmakers expanded the zero tolerance rule to include all manner of drugs and weapons. So now we've got seventh grade girls getting expelled for giving aspirin to friends suffering from menstrual cramps and third grade boys undergoing counseling for drawing pictures of cowboys with guns.

Crazy? Of course.

So let me explain how we got here.

Every school administrator knows that the general public, parents included, wants higher standards and stricter rules in public education. At least, usually they do. But an odd thing happens when it's their kid who gets into trouble. They want understanding. They want leniency. They want an exception. Sometimes, in a case where a student with an impeccable behavior record mouths off to a hall monitor and then is genuinely contrite later, that exception can be warranted.

But it's not always that simple. I heard a story recently about a high school senior who, in a fit of rage, hurled a chair at his math teacher's head, missing it by inches. The boy's mother came to school and insisted that as long as her son apologized, the incident should be forgotten. After all, she said, her son really was "a good kid." And the teacher had made the mistake, after all, of instructing him to sit down and be quiet so that she could begin her class.

Sorry, but any kid who throws a chair, aiming for his teacher's head, is not "a good kid." He's someone with serious anger issues, who needs professional help, fast. Until he gets that help, in my opinion, he shouldn't go anywhere near his math teacher, not to mention his fellow students.

As a result of cases like this one, administrators all over the nation shook their heads in disbelief at the behavior being excused by a few misguided parents (and their lawyers) and came up with the concept of zero tolerance. That made enforcing school rules far simpler and reduced somewhat the incidences of hearing "Oh, come on. Just because there was a machete in his locker didn't mean he actually intended to use it!"

So has zero tolerance gone too far? No doubt. Is it rectifiable? Of course, with a little bit of common sense.

Should you imagine your child getting caught up in the machinations of zero tolerance by bringing a plastic knife to school to portion out a hunk of salami or a wedge of cheese for her buddies at lunchtime, I'd recommend first, an awareness of the current climate before the fact (call it an ounce of prevention; ask her to slice the salami at home the night before) and second, if worse comes to worst, a private talk with your principal after the fact. He or she will probably tell you that the school board policy requires a report on the incident—which is true—but that you are also entitled to a "hearing." That means that the board will review your case behind closed doors after you've had a chance to present your side. Many such suspensions and/or expulsions are overturned this way. In the case of a plastic knife, your board would probably do that. (Your principal may even recommend it.)

That's what generally occurs with the vast majority of those bogus zero tolerance cases. Why don't you ever hear the rest of the story, then?

Easy. It doesn't make a good headline.

On Student Nonperformance and Acting Out

Believe it or not, passivity and aggression are actually flip sides of the same coin. In both cases you've got an angry, frustrated kid, one passive, one aggressive. The passive one has shut down, shows up for school only because she's required to do so by law, but refuses to do any work. ("I'll show you!") She's the one in the back row who slouches, never raises her hand, never turns in a paper, shrugs or closes her eyes when called on or questioned about what her problem is. Many teachers misread this act and take her attitude personally. After all, they can't possibly identify, since they themselves were nearly always such good students! A few become so frustrated by the silent treatment that they give up and just let the kid sleep, both literally and figuratively, thinking that there's no possible way to reach her.

Not true.

Ironically, the aggressive student is actually easier to reach, because his acts are so "out there," with something concrete for a parent or a teacher to address. Aggression is always a sign of fear and/or anger, but that's sometimes difficult to see when you're dealing with your own self-image as a parent, or in the case of a teacher, with one hundred forty-nine other kids! The student with her eyes closed, on the other hand, has built a psychological wall of concrete around herself. Someone must scale it before she becomes her own permanent prisoner.

I'll tell you a little secret about these tough cases. There was never a child born who didn't in his or her heart want to please his or her parents and make them proud. There was never a child born who wouldn't rather be an A student than a failing one. Everyone loves being respected and admired.

Those who decide to fail, sleep, act out all make a conscious or unconscious choice to do so. The reason? Simple. They don't see any possible way to pursue the alternative route and be successful. Somewhere along the line they've become convinced that the work is too hard, it's too much trouble, or they'll never be any good at it anyway.

School is a game they simply cannot win. So they choose not to play.

Or else, they find they get more attention for being troublemakers than well-behaved students. (Imagine the sense of power that comes from being labeled the worst kid in the building!) So they keep on doing what they do best, whatever works for them as far as getting others to pay attention.

The remedy? A positive spotlight, of course. A chance to shine, to be lauded for something other than messing up. This isn't as hard as it sounds. All it takes is a personal relationship with one teacher who genuinely likes him or her—or better yet, the unbeatable combination of parent and teacher, communicating regularly, chatting and laughing over coffee, working together in a friendly rather than adversarial manner. It can literally turn a kid's life around. I've seen it happen countless times.

Think your child's teacher is too busy to take a personal interest in one child—yours?

I think you'd be wrong. In fact, I'd bet on it.

Why not ask and find out? You may find more than one teacher who feels delighted and honored to be chosen.

On Accountability

Many critics have accused educators of not wanting to be held accountable for much of anything. Not so. We definitely want to be held accountable for things that fall under the proper heading of our jobs. Like educating. Like instruction of material. Like searching endlessly for better keys to unlock student learning.

We don't wish to be held accountable for things that are beyond our control. Like parenting! Like whether or not our students can respond politely to a simple request, or whether or not they'll show up every day.

As hard as it is to imagine, one of our biggest problems in public education is spotty attendance. Many schools battle with an uncomfortably large percentage of students who simply aren't there two or three days out of five. Students are kept home for reasons as diverse as "needed to baby-sit younger sister" to "needed to sleep after working late." (Who allowed her to work late? Not her science teacher.) Some districts have even resorted to citing parents to court to combat this disconcerting trend, a pretty sad state of affairs.

So if I'm a principal, yes, go ahead; hold me accountable for whether or not my building is clean, whether or not I'm approachable, returning your phone calls, scheduling enough enrichment assemblies, and for how well my teachers are following the prescribed curriculum of studies. Don't hold me accountable for whether there was enough money in last year's budget to repair the roof or for who got sent to the hospital on Saturday night after a fist fight. (Although you'll probably see me there during visiting hours.)

When we're talking about accountability, the main thing to keep in mind is this: No one can be held accountable for the independent actions of another person. Parents, teachers, and administrators can only work together to give children a set of values which will make them want to excel, both in school and throughout life.

3

How Principals Can Set Up a PIP

Perhaps you're a principal who by now is intrigued and wants to start a Parental Intervention Plan in your own school. (If you're a parent, you'll also find this part interesting, and besides, I'll have more to say to you in a few minutes!) The Plan works best, I've learned, when it follows eight specific steps.

Step 1
Notify personnel.

Let your teachers, your superintendent, and your school board members know that you think you've found a way to create an alliance between the home and the school. You intend to try it, and you need their support. Stress to them that the Plan costs nothing to implement or maintain.

Urge your teachers not to be intimidated by the prospect of an adult audience. It could polish up their performances a bit—and will probably earn them accolades beyond their wildest expectations.

Step 2
Notify parents.

The student who has been a chronic behavior problem should call his parent(s) from the school office to tell them he has been suspended and to explain why. As I've said, this removes the school from the role of adversary. Contrary to popular belief, schools don't set out to suspend students; students get themselves suspended by repeated violations of clearly stated rules. (Parents don't always see it that way, however, until their kids begin to call them with the bad news.)

Step 3
Offer an alternative.

When I finally take the telephone from the student's hand and introduce myself, I explain that because of a new plan, the parent has the option of having the suspension removed—if he'll just come to school and sit with his child for a day. I try to sweeten the deal by making it worth his while: A one-day visit cancels a three-day suspension; two days cancel a five-day suspension.

Step 4
Deal with objections.

Not everyone immediately jumps at the chance. Many parents use the standard bail-out: "I'd like to, but I can't; I work." To which I gently reply that holding down a job doesn't exempt them from the duties of parenting. Then I add that a small investment of time could result in a radical behavioral change. It could even be the deciding factor, in fact, in whether or not the kid ever finishes school! Kids with habitual discipline problems, I point out, frequently become high-school dropouts. Parental influence—and presence—are badly needed. Now.

Finally, I suggest that they run the idea of a school visitation past their boss or supervisor, just to see if perhaps they get more support than they expect.

Then, if all else fails, the parent should take the day off anyway—and take his or her lost wages out of the child's allowance! (No allowance? Try forfeiting the upcoming birthday or Christmas present.) That should certainly make a lasting impression on any teenager.

Step 5
Meet in the office first thing in the morning.

Smile. Shake hands. Tell each parent how delighted you are to see him or her, and how you anticipate good results. Reassure everyone that all they'll be doing in class is observing. (Some parents are genuinely terrified that they'll be called on to read or answer questions. This must not happen!) See that they are escorted to the right rooms and remind them that you'll want to see them again before they leave.

Step 6
Meet again last thing in the afternoon.

This is the best part of the day for any principal. You'll hear how impressed everyone is. I heard compliments on my teachers, on my building's appearance, on the awards prominently displayed, and even on my well-mannered student body!

Occasionally, someone offers a suggestion for building improvement. The smartest thing a principal can do is adopt the idea and then loudly give that person total credit for having come up with it in the first place.

Acknowledge the concern of any parent who feels he or she has witnessed a particularly poor teacher performance that day. Address the issue immediately. You'll gain credibility by doing so, far more than if you try to minimize the problem.

Step 7
Follow up.

This may well be the most important step of all. At some point, a student whose mother or father has come to school "shapes up." Suddenly, he's behaving himself; he's not a familiar face in the office anymore. Call the parents and let them know how pleased the school is, how proud they should be. Then make a regular progress call every two weeks or so, just to reassure them that things are still fine.

If a backslide should occur, it's even more important to follow up and perhaps suggest that one more parental visit might be in order. (You'll rarely be refused.)

Regardless of the follow-up call's purpose, constructive relationships develop. Parents sometimes call my office voluntarily, just to see if their children are continuing to behave.

It gives me genuine pleasure to say yes.

Step 8
Report to personnel.

Pass all compliments about the building, the staff, and the school generally on to your teachers. They've made you look good, and they deserve the credit. After several weeks, present a detailed report to your superintendent and school board, citing numbers of parents in attendance, comments made, and subsequent reductions in student offenses.

Then point out the part with the most impact of all: This procedure has gathered enormous parental support, polished the school's community image, drastically reduced disciplinary problems . . . and it hasn't cost the board of education a red cent.

Now, that certainly ought to get their attention!

Parental intervention works. It works because it gives parents a feeling of power and importance; it works because it gives teachers a feeling of support; it works because it gives schools better public images. And finally, it works because it gives youngsters a very good reason to stay on their best behavior.

Look at it this way: Would you want your mother following you around all day?

4

How Parents Can Initiate a PIP

If you're a parent who believes that intervention would improve your own child's performance, or help other children get back on track, or improve the overall educational experience at the school, here are the steps to take to get things rolling.

Step 1
Make an appointment with your principal to meet face-to-face.

You may be tempted just to communicate by telephone or e-mail, simply because it's quicker and easier, but the personal impact will be lost—and personal impact is what parental intervention is really all about.

Step 2
Smile and act excited.

Reassure your principal that you aren't there to be critical (he or she is bound to wonder). You've just read this neat little book and you think he or she would enjoy hearing about it. Throw in a couple of enticing bits—that the program drastically reduces disciplinary problems, treats teachers and parents as the allies they should become, and that implementation doesn't cost a penny.

If that isn't enough to get an approving nod to your idea, add this bit of statistical information to your pitch: In the year 2000 it cost $40,000/year to house a federal prisoner (less for a state prisoner) and $5,500 to educate a child. There are more than two million prisoners at the state and federal levels, and eighty percent of them are high school dropouts. Obviously, the more children who finish school and go on to lead productive lives, the more money our state and federal governments will save.

Step 3
Be subtle—super salesmanship isn't necessary.

You're not trying to close a deal on a used car. Let the procedure speak for itself. Offer to lend this book, or even to be a test case, if appropriate. This entire first meeting should take ten minutes, tops.

Step 4
Give the principal plenty of time to consider.

You may feel two weeks is more than enough time for a principal to make up his or her mind, but I assure you, it's never that simple. Change is slow. There are all sorts of mitigating factors, along with groups to be canvassed, starting with the school board and central administration (including most notably the superintendent), parent groups, perhaps even teachers' unions. Principals are understandably wary of offending anyone; they can't afford to go in like gangbusters even with what appears to be a sure winner.

Ducks not only need to be lined up in a row; they need to be dressed in their neatly pressed gingham aprons.

Step 5
Under no circumstances should you go over a principal's head.

No matter how tired you get of waiting for a reply, do not go to a higher authority.

There is a hierarchy in school districts that exists for a necessary reason. No superintendent (or school board) wants to be perceived as undermining a principal's authority, just as no principal wants to be charged with the responsibility of running a school without real power of his or her own.

Step 6
Ask for an update on progress.

Continue to be cheery, enthusiastic, and supportive. Keep the atmosphere of your call or meeting light. You're still excited; you hope he or she is too.

Step 7
Deal with objections.

If you encounter objections, be gentle. Remember, principals grow all too accustomed to having their heads on the chopping block and may feel a bit defensive. For example:

"This program hasn't been thoroughly tested."

Yes, it has, by some 20,000 school districts, and those are just the ones I've heard about.

"The teachers won't like being observed by parents." The teachers will change their minds once they find their home-based support skyrocketing.

"Our discipline code works fine just the way it's written."

Not if students are still being suspended. Wouldn't you love to reduce the rate?

"The program just embarrasses the kids."

Only temporarily, and we hope only once; the results are stunningly, staggeringly worthwhile.

Step 8
This is an issue for the peace table, not the battlefield.

Going to battle would undermine the entire philosophy of mutual cooperation. It's possible that your principal will postpone a decision for months. It's possible that he or she will choose not to implement the program this year, but maybe will the next, or the one after that. Or maybe tomorrow three more parents will drop by, waving this slim book and chattering excitedly. You never know. Sometimes offering the name and telephone number of a neighboring administrator who has successfully practiced parental intervention is all it takes. Continue to think positively.

As passionately as I believe in the parent-school alliance, I also know that some things can't be rushed—not before people are ready to accept them. As with all simple ideas, though, someday we'll all wonder why this one took us so long to figure out.

5

How to Participate in a PIP

Nervous? Please try not to be. You're about to embark on one of the most interesting experiences you've ever had. So let me take a few moments to dispel your misgivings by offering these seven easy-to-follow guidelines.

Step 1
Arrive with a positive attitude.

Even if your own educational experience was less than terrific, remember that you're not a kid anymore. This time your principal will be thrilled speechless to have you there. Don't worry, under no circumstances will you be called to account for your child's past sins. This is an intervention, not an inquisition.

Step 2
Don't worry about what your child's teachers will think.

Will you hear, "Oh, there's that terrible mom who can't control her kid and never should have had children to begin with"? No, I don't think so. In fact, I can guarantee that won't be even close to what the other adults are thinking. It will be more like, "Oh, there's a truly caring and courageous parent who's willing to inconvenience herself to guarantee her kid an attitude adjustment and therefore a better shot in life."

Think about the legions of moms and dads, after all, who virtually never come to school, not even when informed that they must do so in order for their children to be reinstated after suspensions.

Feeling better yet?

Step 3
Don't call attention to yourself.

Your presence will be obvious enough; in fact, you'll feel a little like a celebrity. There is no need to feel compelled to announce your entrance or even to introduce yourself. The teacher will take care of that.

Step 4
Watch and listen.

No, not because you need a review on polynomials, but because you, being older and wiser than the rest of the teacher's audience, will pick up on things the kids don't. Like whether the atmosphere in the room feels friendly or dictatorial. Like how hard the teacher is striving to keep her students' attention and whether or not she's succeeding.

Like how difficult it may be for your active seventh grader to sit still all day, every day. (Many adults underestimate how tiring that can be.)

Since teachers have already been briefed not to call on you (or ask you to read aloud), you'll want to refrain from joining in discussions. This may not be easy, especially if you're in possession of some definite convictions—and what adult isn't? But remember, the teacher has a prescribed agenda (it's called a lesson plan), and your story about a great uncle who once met Albert Einstein probably isn't part of it.

On the other hand, a bit of enrichment is good for the soul. If you find yourself bonding with the class, take a look at the teacher's face. If he or she seems relaxed enough to include you in some way, that shouldn't be forbidden. On the other hand, if the teacher is wearing a sour lemon expression or seems to be acting excessively polite and restrained, that may a clue to button up.

Just tread softly here.

Step 5
Communicate your insights
to your principal.

That's the reason for that end-of-the-day meeting, so that the two of you can talk. This is the time to chat, share, ask questions. Why were so many classes empty today? Because this is the last day before Christmas break, and a lot of kids consider it one more day off. Why aren't there more electric fans blowing on such a hot afternoon? Because the school budget isn't sufficient to cover equipment like that, and if fans are whirring away, it's because the teachers probably paid for them out of their own pockets.

I do hope you'll have some positive things to say. I would be genuinely surprised if you didn't. People in the abstract tend to put down public schools, but once they spend a day inside one, they're painfully aware of the many hurdles we must all overcome. Like not enough time, energy, or resources.

What should you do, then, if you wind up at the day's end convinced more than ever that your child is telling the truth when she claims that Mrs. Sweeney's class is b-o-r-i-n-g? Or that nobody likes her? Isn't this a good time, now that you have the principal's ear, to demand that little Shelley be transferred to the class of one of your school's more glowing performers?

In a word, no. As much as I'd like to say that all teachers are stars, we know that it's not true. The world is filled with perfectly competent people who are struggling to be the best they can be and finding it a consistently uphill battle. It has been said that if you have one truly gifted teacher in a lifetime, you're lucky. The good news is, one is all it takes.

The other good news is that your child will need to learn at some point that not every boss or supervisor will be bursting with talent or exciting enough to change his or her life for the better. Eventually, your child will even be required to take orders from someone he or she doesn't particularly like! Being exposed to and dealing with different personalities, not all of whom he or she will be crazy about, is an important life skill.

If you encounter a teacher who really is terrible, bring up the problem with the principal in private. You'll need to establish a couple of things: First, that you aren't on a mission to annihilate someone's career just because he or she gave your child a D. (Don't laugh; it happens.) Second, that you have serious cause to believe that this person should definitely not be working with children. (Generally, we're talking about someone who is prone to shows of temper or who makes unreasonable demands or who is teaching outright fallacies or who has absolutely no clue how to motivate young people.)

Submit your evidence. Be as specific as you can. Ask the principal to investigate (he or she surely will) and then get back to you.

Be aware that unless a teacher is on a limited contract, a dismissal is tough. Tough, but not impossible. The principal must build a case, extend due process, give the teacher a reasonable chance to improve. Many do. Some do not. Termination does happen, despite what you may have read from anti-teachers-union columnists.

But I won't kid you. It takes time. The thing to keep in mind is that secretly the principal may be grateful to you for having brought the matter to his or her attention. Principals don't care to warehouse incompetents in their schools any more than parents do. To rectify such situations, however, particularly in the cases of tenured teachers, they need to establish a solid foundation in order to proceed.

One final note: If you suspect that a teacher is actually doing something illegal or immoral, then you have a right to expect immediate action (probably a suspension) and a thorough investigation. I feel certain that you'll get it. No principal can afford, either financially or professionally, to tap dance around the "feelings" of a fellow adult who may be abusing kids or tinkering with the law.

Step 6
Remain calm and don't
overreact at home.

Once you and Shelley walk through the front door, it will be difficult to resist making a long speech to the little culprit. Probably something along the lines of, "If you ever do anything to embarrass me like that again, I'll . . ." Trust me. Stay off your soapbox. Whatever you vent in anger will accomplish nothing and perhaps result in long-lasting damage. Besides, there's a better way to be effective.

To your child, you need to say only one thing: "I admire the way you handled my being there." That's it. Resist any impulses to elaborate. Say it once, and then forget it. If you talk too much, you'll kill the message, which is, "You don't ever want to have a day like that again."

Step 7
Spread the word.

If you've seen good things happening in your school (and you will), people working hard, students and teachers getting along, a lesson on molecules that turned out to be pretty interesting, don't keep it to yourself. Tell your friends, your minister, your neighbors, your know-it-all brother-in-law. So many people put down our schools. Yet they often haven't set foot inside one in decades.

You have. You know the truth. Now it's time to share it.

6

A Principal's Rules for Parenting Teens

I've had the chance over many years to observe a variety of parenting styles, many successful, some less so. While we can all agree that there is no definitively "right" way to rear a child, I also think it is safe to make the following recommendations. These nuggets are based on what I have repeatedly witnessed regarding children ages eleven to eighteen over the last thirty years as a teacher, principal, and school superintendent.

Never do anything for a child that he can do for himself.

Are you still packing his lunch? Making his bed? Doing his laundry? What would it take for you to rethink that?

How about this: You're reinforcing dependence. You're guaranteeing that he'll learn nothing except how to count on someone else to do his chores, not a positive quality in anyone, certainly not in a grown person of twenty-five. You heard me. Do you still want him living with you into adulthood, still expecting to be fed, clothed, and housed at your expense? It happens.

On the other hand, every time a teenager begs to be allowed to run his own life, as long as the request is reasonable, I'd let him. And with that goes the financial responsibility too.

Allow her to make mistakes.

That's how we all learn. Say your fourteen-year-old wants to buy a pricey new blouse. You take one look and want to hold your nose. First, it's ugly. Second, it will fall apart the first time she washes it. What do you do?

I hope you keep silent and just smile.

There's a terrific opportunity for some education here. Your daughter spends three weeks' worth of her fast food money on the blouse. In less than a month she finds it's gaudy, out of style, ripping apart at every seam. What do you do?

Keep silent and smile.

Next time, she'll be smarter. And you haven't deprived her of the learning experience.

Let him suffer the consequences.

A simple detention, and some parents sweep in, wings flapping like overprotective geese, demanding that the punishment be rescinded because the teacher was "picking" on their child. Well, in my experience teachers rarely have the time to pick on anyone; all they're praying for is a quiet, uneventful day.

And so what if three kids were prancing around the room, and yours was the only one told to stay after class for a quiet talk? Maybe the teacher sees more potential in him. Maybe she wants him to set an example for the others. And in a worst-case scenario, okay, maybe the treatment was less than democratic. Do you really believe you'll be around to protect your child from every unfair sling and arrow hurled at him?

I see this as a terrific chance to tell him how proud you are of how he handles life's rougher moments. Refrain from bailing him out so that he can learn.

Restrain the impulse to overindulge.

How's this for a scenario? Tommy turns sixteen. Mom and Dad buy him a car. Tommy wrecks it. Mom and Dad buy him another car. He wrecks that one. Mom and Dad buy him. . . .

You think I'm kidding, don't you? Unfortunately, I'm not. Yes, we all love our children, and we want to give them as much as we possibly can—but overindulgence is a form of abuse. Sooner or later Tommy will have to support himself, and will he ever be mad when he learns not only that things must be earned, but that the nicer the things, the more work they take.

And when he wrecks his car? The police aren't likely to buy him a new one. Nor is the owner of the truck he just hit.

Commiserate with your child.

Lest you think I recommend a hard-nosed approach in all instances of child-rearing, consider this: Every time your child launches into a speech about how hard her life is, spare her your own stories about having to walk to school six miles in the snow, uphill, both ways. There is no way our kids will ever understand what it was like having only three channels on flickering black-and-white televisions, anymore than we can comprehend having our families marched off to work camps. So don't put yourself in the role of adversary by reminding your daughter of how lucky she is to have a used car to drive, when all you had was a bike!

Tell her you love her, you wish that you could give her the moon tied with a red ribbon—but first, you can't afford it, and second, you know that it wouldn't be good for her anyway, because then she'd ask for the sun.

Hug her, and tell her you've decided to build her character instead.

Choose your battles wisely.

Drugs, gangs, guns, alcohol, early marriage and/or pregnancy, keeping one's grades up, staying out of trouble with the law and the school—those are all reasonable things for parents to take a stand on. I'm not sure that bizarre styles of dress or colors of hair fall into the same category.

Besides, dressing in a way that annoys adults is a rite of passage. Every younger generation has done it, and every older generation has shaken its collective head in horror. (Get out your own high school yearbook or prom picture if you want a good chuckle.)

This is not to say that schools shouldn't have regulations against kids coming to school with blue hair. How would you like to be the teacher trying to get a class's attention when someone walks in looking like an Easter egg? Freedom of expression, when it comes to body piercing, droopy drawers, halter tops, and the like, begins at 3:00 p.m.

Still, if I had to choose between taking a stand against my son wearing a nose stud when he's out with his friends and keeping my relationship with him healthy, I think I'd choose the latter. This is a decision that you'll have to make yourself, of course, but remember, if you pick a fight about everything, you'll win on nothing. Not every single issue should become a major battlefield.

Clothing and hair seem to me like fairly reasonable (and very temporary) ways for kids to rebel. Besides, some tattoo remover somewhere will be doing a booming business about ten years from now.

Skip the lecture.

After about the second sentence of your tirade, your kids won't even hear you. If you begin with, "How many times have I told you," or worse, "When I was your age," they'll tune you out faster than a mayonnaise commercial. Rather than the paragraph, try to master the one-liner.

Like: "I don't think so" in response to "Mom, can Billy and I hitchhike to California and live on the beach next June?"

This one is worth practicing in front of a mirror if necessary.

Feel free to say, "I'll think about it" or "Tell me more."

A favorite beating-down tactic of adolescents is telling a parent, "I need an answer NOW."

No, they don't. They want an answer NOW, because it raises the likelihood of their getting to yes. Catch Mom when she's trying to put a five-course holiday dinner on the table or Dad when he's walking through the door carrying seven bags of groceries and that spring break trip to Florida is theirs!

Never be afraid to buy yourself some time. Don't succumb to the put-downs about "old people" who think too slowly or the emotional blackmail of "You don't trust me." You have a right to talk to other parents, find out who else is going, what the chaperone situation will be. It's

also not a bad idea to teach your kids that the more information you have, the more likely you are to grant their
requests.

Be patient.

You don't approach teenagers. They approach you.
Understand that heart-to-heart talks occur on their time,
not yours.

Ask, "How was school today?" and you'll probably get
a mere shrug. But saunter out to the garage while your
son is working on his car, hang around, ask a question
about that air filter, and you may just get lucky. He might
mention the girl he's trying to get up the nerve to call. He
might even ask for your advice! Just don't rapid-fire too
many questions. To him, it will feel like an interrogation.

Also, be prepared for the fact that teenagers have an
interesting tendency to liven up and get chatty around
midnight. It's their version of the biological clock. Stifle
your yawns, grin and bear it, and thank your lucky stars
that they're still happily yammering away—to you!—into
the wee hours.

Never forget who's really in charge.

You are. Legally, financially, and morally. All of that stuff
you hear about the peer group being the most important
influence in your child's life is true only to a point. Yes,
the peer group's impact is significant, but it's also fleeting.
You'll still be in your child's life long after best buddy Ben
and soul mate Suzy have gone to college, joined the
Navy, or had twins. Your emotional support and approval
are far more essential to your children than they will ever
admit. And what's more, it will continue to be so for their
entire lives.

Questions and Answers for Principals

Here are fifteen common questions I've been asked by principals and other school administration personnel since I developed the PIP.

1
Why do you feel that your parental intervention plan works so well?

Because it's the best combination of forces we can marshal: Parents, teachers, and administrators, all working together to turn kids into better citizens.

I've seen kids from households where the parents spoke no English striving to do their best and ending up with As and Bs. On the other hand, I've seen bright kids with 130 IQs failing all of their subjects and repeatedly getting suspended from school.

What makes the difference? I believe it has always been and still is parental involvement.

2
Do parents ever refuse to come to school?

Occasionally, but not very often. Most are eager to do whatever they can to boost the educational process. The three-for-one deal is a terrific enticement; nobody wants a thirteen-year-old home alone on an unmonitored suspension for three days, doing heaven-knows-what.

Remind reluctant parents that parenting, as everyone knows, is the hardest job in the world. Parents get no money-back guarantees and rarely any thanks. They can invest dollars, time, energy, and stress units into child-rearing—and still wind up completely dissatisfied with the results.

Or they can get lucky—and wind up feeling prouder than they'd ever imagined. The parents who take the time to find out what's going on in their child's school, who monitor homework assignments, who show up for conferences when asked, are far more likely to wind up with disciplined, responsible youngsters than those who don't.

3
What happens when a parent does refuse?

I ask him or her to consider that a few hours of time could change the child's performance in school for the better, and that change could last years. (Remind the parents that eighty percent of federal and state prisoners are high school dropouts.) For those who insist that their bosses won't allow them a day off to come to school, I make a simple suggestion: Ask.

It's my opinion that most people are vitally interested in improving our schools. Many bosses, I think, would be fascinated by the idea of parents going to school for a day, and would even want to hear all about the experience afterward.

4
Isn't this just an updated version of "Wait 'till your father gets home"?

Probably. But I remember a time when a kid who got into trouble at school got into even more at home. That's one return to the good old days that I favor.

5
Isn't this tactic of embarrassing the kid hitting below the belt for most easily traumatized adolescents?

Well, I still cherish the memory of the daughter who tried to push her mother's buttons by proclaiming, "You're embarrassing me!" The mother gave her the perfect answer: "Well, you embarrass me every time you act up."

Remember, humiliation isn't the goal here; refocusing is. And this powerful tool generally only needs to be used once. Also, if you really want to see embarrassment, try dealing with a child who drops out of school at age sixteen because nobody taught him that he couldn't always have his way back when he was twelve. Imagine being that same kid at age twenty, deciding to go back and finish school and wishing fervently that his mom or dad had been gutsy enough to stand up to him.

6
How do you enlist the support of your superintendent and school board members?

By keeping them informed every step of the way of plans, possible outcomes, and eventual results. Regular reports do wonders for encouraging supportive attitudes.

7
Don't teachers resent the intrusion of parents in their classrooms?

Not if they're good. The best teachers are proud of what they do every day, and they welcome the chance to show off a little. I think they deserve that opportunity. If you have a teacher who objects too strenuously to the notion of parental visits, take a closer look. You might find he or she has something to hide.

8
But isn't a class (or even a teacher) on its best behavior when visitors are present?

So what's wrong with that?

9
Does that best behavior truly provide an accurate picture of what's going on in your school?

Over time, yes. No one can keep an act going forever. After a while everyone relaxes and gets on with business as usual. That's the beauty of parental intervention. Parents really do see education in action, and they learn firsthand that teaching isn't the easy job so many think it is.

10
So . . . how do you begin the plan?

With one student and one parent. Take a child who's been in trouble repeatedly and who's consistently refused to mend his ways. Call his father or mother. Cheerfully invite him or her to spend a day with the child, sitting through all of his classes in lieu of a suspension. Notify your school board members that you're trying a little experiment. Then sit back and watch what happens.

11
What does happen?

The effect on the student by the day's end will be stunning beyond belief. Typically, he or she will be very shaken by the grins and remarks endured from friends. Typically, the child will do almost anything to make sure he or she never has that kind of day again—even behave!

12
And the parent?

The effect on the parent is even more profound. As I've said, he or she is generally shocked to discover how exhausting teaching school can be. Most parents have never had the chance to watch teachers for an entire day, so the result is a new respect for educators. Todd the Troublemaker's mother wasn't the only one to say to me at the first day's end, "I think all of your teachers deserve pay increases!"

13
What happens next?

Use this plan with three troublesome students in a row, and the word will spread through your school like a forest fire. You'll sense a difference almost immediately; even the hallways during class changes will seem quieter.

14
Why?

Because no teenager wants his or her mother following him or her around all day! The greatest of all deterrents to teenage misbehavior is embarrassment in front of their friends. If a kid will step in front of a roaring freight train to avoid being taunted by his buddies, then imagine how far he'll go to avoid having his mommy sitting next to him in math class.

15
Does this method ever fail?

I haven't seen it happen yet, although in the instance of the first boy on whom I used the plan, his mother had to come to school three times. Only when she threatened to sit with him for the rest of the year did he finally settle down. But I consider that boy an extreme case.

8

Questions and Answers for Parents

Here are ten common questions parents ask me about the PIP.

1

I've talked myself blue in the face about the importance of education. Yet my fourteen-year-old continues to ignore me, slack off, and misbehave. And you're trying to convince me that one visit to his school can turn his attitude around?

Yes, I am. I'm afraid you have made a common parental error: Talking too much, rather than too little. Real power consists of quick action, not long speeches. Our kids may tune us out, but they can't ignore what we do. One day-long visit to your child's school, following your child to each of his classes, will make more of an impression than hours of emotional tirades.

2

I think I have a bad case of school phobia left over from the tenth grade. Every time I walk into a school building, I start to sweat. Any advice?

That school phobia is not as rare as you might think; it might be one reason that more parents don't attend conferences. First, I can promise that no one will ask you to produce a hall pass, issue you a detention, or refuse to let you use the restroom. Second, you might try a small taste before having to consume the entire six-course dinner. Walk through a school on a Saturday morning when weekend activities are taking place and promise yourself that you need stay only five minutes. Then see if you can increase the time to ten minutes without getting heart palpitations. Another remedy is to find a teacher, any teacher, and cultivate a friendship with him or her. That will help school personnel seem far more human.

3

This parental intervention experience will probably leave me bursting with insights. What if the principal doesn't have time to meet with me at the end of the day?

Unless the school is ablaze, he or she will. Nobody in a high-pressure job filled with constant criticism will turn down a chance to hear good things! Even if there is plaster falling on somebody's head in the cafeteria, and he or she has to attend to it immediately, you can be sure that you'll receive a heartfelt apology and a timely phone call at home. A sudden crisis is nothing personal, I assure you. It's part of a principal's normal day.

4

I'm having trouble believing that you really visited every classroom several times each day. How large was your school, and who did your paperwork?

Believe it. I made being accessible my highest priority. In many cases, I didn't need to stay in a classroom long; often I just ducked my head in, looked around, and then moved on. But I found that doing this actually saved me time in the long run because I always heard people's concerns immediately and could jot them down on the spot. Also, I began my day early, about six o'clock and went home about five in the evening, and then returned for evening activities. Paperwork, always an ugly demon, was delegated as much as possible—which is as it should be.

As for size of school, my junior high (middle school) had 800 students and the high school where I was principal a few years later had close to 2,000. By the way, I believe the days of schools with huge enrollments will soon be a thing of the past. Studies show that kids don't feel cared for or known unless they are in much smaller groups. The largest size that seems to work well for kids is about 500 students.

5

My boss absolutely refuses to consider letting me off work to go to my child's school, even for one day. What do I do now?

Keep trying. Offer to take a sick day, a personal day, or a vacation day. Take a day off without pay. Make up a day on your regular day off. Offer to take the boss with you—everyone has a vested interest in the success of all of our children. If your boss is really that uncooperative where your child's education is concerned, ask yourself what sort of medieval work environment issues you're tolerating in other areas.

6

How many times will I have to do this PIP before my child changes?

Generally, you only have to go to school with your child once, although you may not believe me until you try it. Rest assured that no self-respecting adolescent wants daddy sitting with him all day in school. Once is horrible enough. Two or three times would be social suicide. Remember, though, that you need to go with your child to every class and stay for the whole school day.

7

I worry about embarrassing my child. I'm reluctant to put him (or her) in such a vulnerable position in front of his friends. Isn't that cruel and unusual treatment?

Not when you consider the stakes: Finishing school or not finishing school; getting serious about education or not getting serious; having a successful, productive life or continuing to be a master manipulator who thinks he or she doesn't need to follow the same rules as everyone else. Think about it.

8

Speaking of vulnerable, how will I face my friends at church or work when they hear that I had to spend the day sitting with my misbehaving twelve-year-old?

Don't sneak out the back, Jack. Don't make a new plan, Fran. The best defense is a good offense. You tell everyone long before the grapevine goes to work. Brag about it! You're a concerned parent who took a drastic but laudable action. And now you have an insider's view of how school works, not to mention the principal's home telephone number. You'll leave a lot of parents feeling envious of your courageous action, although it may take them a while to admit it.

9

You say that once my child and I get back home, I shouldn't make any long speeches. Well, I haven't had the chance—my son hasn't spoken to me in four days. How much longer will the silent treatment go on?

Until your son needs something, such as fast food money or a ride somewhere. As painful as it is to admit, he's trying to punish you, make you sorry that you were ever born, let alone sitting next to him in health class. For a time, he may even succeed. But you don't have to let him know he's gotten to you.

Continue to resist any impulse to make a speech or to explain your point of view. (He doesn't think you have one.) Go about your business. Act cheerful. Whistle. He'll thaw out by Christmas. In the meantime, you won't have to wonder if you've made the proper impression. You have!

10

How can I tell if my child is attending a good school?

That depends on what you mean by "good." You can consider standardized test scores or the number of college-bound students if you wish. I personally would rather hear about a well-structured discipline code (that supports teachers teaching and students learning) and a mobile, approachable principal. After that, I'd talk to the teachers: Are they glad to be there? Are they excited about their profession and about kids? Do they respect and feel supported by their administrators?

Then, of course, I'd check with my child and other students: Do they enjoy coming to school? Are they comfortable around their principal? Can they talk to their teachers? Do they feel the building belongs to them?

For any school to be considered "good," people have to feel reasonably happy to be there and structured, progressive learning must be taking place.

And finally, the school's discipline code should include some form of effective parental intervention!

9

Backing It Up

As a junior high and high school principal (and now as superintendent of an award-winning alternative school for at-risk youth, selected as the best in the state of Ohio two years in a row), I've had the opportunity to observe many different parenting styles. They range from the over-protective kind that forbids even healthy socializing with peers to the indifferent kind that responds to my "I'd like to talk about your son Chris," with a befuddled "Who?"

What makes the difference? I believe it always was and still is parental involvement.

The reason is simple: The kids receive a clear message about who's in charge. They have virtually no recourse against the combined power of parents, teachers, and administrators. It's only when they perceive a rift in that triumvirate that they start playing one against the other. Then we adults learn the true meaning of "divide and conquer."

You may already have heard of Temple University psychologist Lawrence Steinberg, who published the results of an exhaustive study of school-age children and teenagers in *Beyond the Classroom: Why School Reform Has Failed and What Parents Need to Know* (1996). Steinberg sought to find out why so many kids these days are "disengaged" from learning. He explored many variables, including socio-economic and ethnic backgrounds.

Steinberg discovered (no surprise to me) that what makes the most critical difference is parental involvement. But not the kind you'd expect, not the nightly checking of homework and periodic offering of verbal encouragement—but the kind that draws parents physically onto the school grounds.

"When parents take the time to attend a school function—time off from an evening activity or . . . from their own jobs—they send a strong message about how important school is to them and, by extension, how important it should be to the child," Steinberg explains. "It reinforces in the child's mind that school and home are connected. [And] teachers cannot help but pay closer attention to students whose parents they encounter frequently at school programs."

He goes on to say that when successful students do encounter obstacles, their parents immediately show up on the school's doorstep to "mobilize the school on their child's behalf—they 'work the system.' It lets the school know that they expect [it] to serve their child." This kind of attention to their child's success in school is within the grasp of every parent who is willing to invest the time.

James Levine, director of The Fatherhood Project at the Families and Work Institute in New York City, notes in *Working Fathers: New Strategies for Balancing Work and Family* (1997) that "nowhere is the power of your [fathers and mothers both] connection with the other important adults in your child's life more compelling than in your child's education." Other adults? That would mean, of course, teachers and principals. According to Levine, even the youngest school-age children spend about 60% of their waking hours away from their parents. All the more vital, then, that parents and school personnel forge a positive alliance.

And while we're on the subject, Tom Loveless, director of the Brown Center on Educational Policy at the Brookings Institution in Washington, D.C. says this: "The family is the single, most important influence when it comes to learning. Peer values are strong—but adult values are stronger." It's our business to make certain they stay that way.

Expect the best from your child, and work with his or her teachers and administrators to ensure that you get it. Start by calling your child's school and asking if you might drop by for an hour to visit some classrooms and to chat with the principal. In this day and age you may encounter some amazement, but little resistance. Most principals will fall all over themselves to make you feel welcome.

Then suggest implementing a parental intervention plan that would involve more parents, promote a more positive image of the school, and create a more effective disciplinary climate for youngsters.

In order for schools to gain a higher and better profile, parents have to witness firsthand what is happening—and then they have to talk about it. In order for education to be truly effective, the school and the home must work together.

It's just that simple.

Reflections on Being Educators

John Lazares

I grew up in Hamilton, Ohio, a blue-collar community just north of Cincinnati. My mother was a teacher. My younger sister Chris and I were taught from birth the tremendous value of an education.

When I graduated from Miami University in Oxford, Ohio, I returned to my own hometown to teach like many of my classmates. Hamilton may well hold the world's record as far as its number of classroom teachers who are also its alumni. That's why you'll so often see kids in school libraries huddled over old yearbooks, pointing and giggling.

I earned a Master's degree almost immediately and then became an assistant principal and soon afterward a principal. As a principal I developed the Parental Intervention Plan. It went "public" in 1990. Since then, I've received literally thousands of letters and phone calls from parents, teachers, and administrators eager to try something similar in their local school districts. I'm pleased to report that approximately 20,000 school districts nationwide have successfully put the PIP into practice.

I'm often asked if my program works better with some grade levels or socio-economic levels than with others. That's what makes it so amazing. It works with first graders, with seniors in high school, and everyone in between. I do feel that its maximal impact, though, is felt in grades six through ten, since those ages are when young people are most sensitive to what their friends will say and think.

As for the economic aspect, the city of Hamilton, although a very attractive small city of approximately 60,000, is as far away from being "Pleasantville, U.S.A." as anywhere you'll find. It has the twelfth largest school district in Ohio, with a heavy volume of special needs and at-risk kids. The wealthier west side is a mere five-minute drive from subsidized housing, and students from all neighborhoods sit side-by-side in their English classes. The high school sees about 45% of its student body on free or reduced-price lunches. One local elementary school found their free-lunch ratio so substantial, around 95%, that they finally figured it would be cheaper and easier to feed everyone, rather than mess with the paperwork. Still, Hamilton feels strongly that diversity is one of its greatest assets, and I would agree. It was, therefore, an ideal test case for a parental intervention plan.

I have since become superintendent of the Warren County Educational Service Center in Lebanon, Ohio, with an administrative career having spanned twenty-seven years so far. I still believe that all schools and all students have one thing in common: When concerned parents get involved, failure is impossible. When parents, teachers, and administrators work together, children are invariably successful, and, as a result, far happier.

Coleen Armstrong

When I was a child, my mother used to warn me, "Be anything you want to be—only, please, don't be a teacher." (She had briefly taught school herself in the early 1940s.) Imagine, then, both of our surprise, when at age sixteen I was sitting in English class—and I heard a command from the universe. I knew instantly what I was destined to do with my life, or at least the first half of it.

In 1968 I followed my then-fiancé from Cleveland to Hamiltion, Ohio (where I later met John Lazares). Thirty-one years later, I was still there, having logged extensive experience teaching English, German, and Spanish, grades seven through twelve, both junior high and high school.

I'd been blessed that first year to have been assigned an exceptionally gifted group of bright and brash fifteen-year-olds who opened their hearts to me via journal writing. Because they let their guards down, I did too—and thus learned very early the most important teaching lesson: Young people, like all humans, are intricate mixtures of vulnerability and bravado, confidence and self-deprecation. Every child secretly longs to be successful and to make his or her parents proud. A youth just sometimes needs help figuring out how best to do it. John Lazares's Parental Intervention Plan speaks directly to that issue.

There seem to be two separate tiers in public education today. The first is comprised of the college-bound, let's-set-the-world-on-fire kids who would probably learn even if locked in a dark closet. Second, the under-achievers who are fed up with sitting in a classroom and want nothing more than to finish high school as quickly as possible. The first group nearly always has hands-on, involved parents. The second group rarely does. That should tell us something.

The secret to any school's success is incredibly simple: Parental backup. Over thirty-one years I sat across many a kitchen table, sipping coffee, happily trading personal histories with moms and dads—and the positive effect on my students was nothing short of astonishing. Parents and teachers working together. . . . Wow, what a concept! So easy, yet so impactful. And what's more, it's what all of us, parents, teachers, and even our kids really want.

Index

Practical Books for Thoughtful Parents from Parenting Press

Grounded for Life?! Stop Blowing Your Fuse and Start Communicating with Your Teenager by Louise Felton Tracy, M.A. School counselor and mother of six shows parents how to turn unproductive, unpleasant years with teens into growth-filled, satisfying years. Warm and understanding, the author shares learning experiences from her own family and the middle schoolers in her life. Useful with ages 10-18 years. 164 pages. $12.95 paperback. **Parents' Choice Award.**

Understanding Temperament: Strategies for Creating Family Harmony by Lyndall Shick, M.A. When parents know why family members behave as they do, and how to manage their behavior, they can change family conflict and misunderstanding into cooperation and compassion. Many strategies offered for coping with different temperament types. Useful with all ages. 126 pages. $13.95 paperback.

Pick Up Your Socks . . . and Other Skills Growing Children Need! A Practical Guide to Raising Responsible Children by Elizabeth Crary, M.S. Responsibility is a skill parents can teach. Whether it's teaching a small child to pick up his socks or a teenager to handle peer pressure, parents will find an abundance of real-life examples, complete with consequences. Author helps parents be realistic in their expectations through discussions of developmental stages and learning styles. Includes chart showing when kids can reasonably be expected to remember to feed the pet, take out the trash, do laundry, cook a meal, etc. Useful with ages 3-15 years. 112 pages. $14.95 paperback.

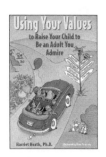

Using Your Values to Raise Your Child to Be an Adult You Admire by Harriet Heath, Ph.D. All parents have values, but few consider them when dealing with everyday situations, or think about how their values may affect their children years down the road. Author helps parents identify what they want for their children in the long term and shows them how to plant the seeds of future success early on. Thought-provoking book. Useful with all ages. 176 pages. $16.95 paperback.

Prices subject to change without notice

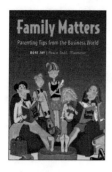

Family Matters: Parenting Tips from the Business World by Roni Jay. What are the advantages to using business skills within families? This helpful and enjoyable book looks at parenting with the eye of a manager who knows how to acknowledge "customer" needs, sell benefits, negotiate everything from toddler bedtimes to teenage curfews, pick incentives that really work with kids, and motivate siblings to work as a team. Useful with all ages. 128 pages. $13.95 paperback.

**For a complete catalog of books
by Parenting Press, please contact:**

Parenting Press, Inc.
P.O. Box 75267 / Seattle, Washington 98125
Toll free 1-800-992-6657

In Canada, call Raincoast Books Distribution Company
1-800-663-5714

**For weekly parenting tips, book descriptions,
author information, and more, please see:**

www.ParentingPress.com